BALI TRAVEL GUIDE 2023

Discover the Hidden Gems of Bali: A Comprehensive Travel Guide for Adventure, Culture, and Relaxation

Lawrence A. Hurd

All rights reserved. No part of this publication may be reproduced, distributed, or transmitted in any form or by any means, including photocopying, recording, or other electronic or mechanical methods, without the prior written permission of the publisher, except in the case of brief quotations embodied in critical reviews and certain other noncommercial uses permitted by copyright law.

Copyright © Lawrence Hurd, 2023.

Table of contents

My trip to Bali
Welcome to Bali
Introduction

Chapter 1: "The Ultimate Bali Travel Guide: 5 Things You Need to Know Before You Go"
Best time to visit Bali
Entry requirements for Bali
Passport Requirements:
Visa Requirements:
COVID-19 Requirements:
Other Requirements:
Currency and exchange rates in Bali
Language and culture in Bali
Cultural practices to keep in mind when traveling to Bali:
Safety tips for traveling to Bali

Chapter 2: "Discover Bali: 5 Must-Visit Places on Your Trip"
Ubud: Cultural Heart of Bali
Kuta, the surfing paradise
Seminyak, the trendy beach town
Nusa Penida, the island paradise
Tanah Lot Temple, the iconic Bali landmark

Chapter 3: "Bali on a Budget: 5 Tips for Traveling to Bali on a Shoestring"
Affordable accommodations in Bali
Cheap eats in Bali
Free or low-cost activities in Bali
How to negotiate prices in Bali
Budget-friendly transportation options in Bali

Chapter 4: "The Ultimate Foodie's Guide to Bali: 5 Must-Try Dishes"
Nasi Goreng, the national dish of Indonesia
Babi Guling, Bali's famous suckling pig
Sate, Indonesian-style grilled meat skewers
Gado-gado, a salad of mixed vegetables and peanut sauce
Lawar, a traditional Balinese dish made with minced meat and spices

Chapter 5: "Relax and Recharge: 5 Best Wellness Retreats in Bali"
COMO Shambhala Estate, Ubud
The Yoga Barn, Ubud
Fivelements, Mambal
Bali Silent Retreat, Tabanan
Svarga Loka Resort, Ubud

Chapter 6: "Off the Beaten Path: 5 Hidden Gems in Bali Worth Exploring"

Tirta Gangga, a stunning water palace
Jatiluwih Rice Terraces, a UNESCO World Heritage Site
Tenganan Village, a preserved Balinese village
Pura Lempuyang, a temple with breathtaking views
Menjangan Island, a diving and snorkeling paradise

Chapter 7: "Bali with Kids: 5 Fun Family-Friendly Activities"
Bali Safari and Marine Park, Gianyar
Waterbom Bali, Kuta
Bali Treetop Adventure Park, Bedugul:
Bali Bird Park, Gianyar:
Green Camp Bali, Ubud:

Chapter 8: "Bali's Nightlife Scene: 5 Hotspots for a Night Out"
Potato Head Beach Club, Seminyak
Sky Garden, Kuta
La Favela, Seminyak
Single Fin, Uluwatu

Chapter 9: "Romantic Bali: 5 Activities for Couples"
Sunset dinner at Jimbaran Bay
Sunrise hike to Mount Batur
Couples massage at a luxury spa
Private Villa with a Pool:
Scenic Helicopter Tour of Bali:

Chapter 10: The Best Souvenirs to Bring Home from Bali: 5 Must-Buy Items.

Batik textiles and clothing

Handmade jewelry and accessories

Traditional Balinese masks and puppets

Coffee and spices from Bali

Hand-carved wooden souvenirs and home decor.

My trip to Bali

My trip to Bali began with a flight into the island's only international airport, Ngurah Rai International Airport, located in the southern part of Bali. Upon arriving, I was immediately struck by the natural beauty of the island. The warm tropical air, lush green forests, and crystal-clear waters were a feast for the senses.

One of the first places I visited in Bali was Kuta Beach, a long stretch of golden sand that is a popular spot for surfing and sunbathing. The beach was crowded with tourists, but there was still plenty of space to relax and soak up the sun. I rented a surfboard and took to the waves, enjoying the warm water and gentle swells.

After a day at Kuta Beach, I traveled to Ubud, a town located in the central part of Bali. Ubud is known for its artistic and cultural heritage and is home to many museums, galleries, and traditional markets. I visited the Ubud Monkey

Forest, a nature reserve and Hindu temple complex that is home to hundreds of macaque monkeys. The monkeys were friendly and curious, and I enjoyed watching them play and interact with each other.

One of the highlights of my trip to Bali was visiting the rice terraces in Tegalalang, a village located north of Ubud. The rice terraces are a UNESCO World Heritage site and are famous for their unique irrigation system, which has been used for centuries to grow rice. I hiked through the terraces, marveling at the intricate network of canals and the stunning views of the surrounding hills and forests.

Another must-visit attraction in Bali is the Tanah Lot temple, a Hindu shrine located on a rocky outcropping in the sea. The temple is one of the most popular tourist destinations in Bali and is especially beautiful at sunset, when the orange and pink hues of the sky blend with the blue of the sea to create a breathtaking vista. I watched as locals and tourists alike gathered to pay their respects to the gods and take in the stunning views.

One of the things I loved most about Bali was the food. Balinese cuisine is known for its use of fresh, local ingredients and its emphasis on bold flavors and spices. I sampled everything from nasi goreng (fried rice) to satay (grilled meat skewers) to sambal (spicy chili sauce). One of my favorite meals was at a small warung (local eatery) in Ubud, where I had a delicious bowl of mie goreng (fried noodles) and a refreshing glass of es kelapa (coconut ice).

In addition to its natural beauty and cultural attractions, Bali is also a great destination for relaxation which makes the best tourism view.
In all, visiting Bali will automatically be one of the countries you will cherish to revisit again .

Welcome to Bali

Bali is a beautiful island in Indonesia that offers an abundance of natural beauty, unique culture, and exciting activities. It is known for its picturesque rice terraces, stunning beaches, and serene temples that attract millions of tourists every year.

Upon arriving in Bali, you will be greeted with warm hospitality and friendly locals who are eager to share their culture and traditions with you. The island is famous for its vibrant festivals and ceremonies, which are held regularly throughout the year. From the Nyepi Day of Silence to the Galungan Festival, these events offer a glimpse into the island's rich heritage and customs.

One of the most popular activities in Bali is surfing. The island is home to some of the best surf breaks in the world, and attracts surfers from all over the globe. Whether you are a beginner or an experienced surfer, there are plenty of spots to catch a wave and soak up the sun. Bali is also an excellent place for diving and snorkeling, with clear waters and a diverse marine ecosystem.

For those seeking a more relaxed vacation, Bali offers plenty of opportunities for rejuvenation and wellness. The island is renowned for its spa treatments, yoga retreats, and meditation centers, where you can unwind and recharge your batteries. Many of these wellness activities are set against a backdrop of stunning natural scenery, making for a truly immersive and rejuvenating experience.

Bali is also a food lover's paradise, with a rich culinary scene that draws on the island's diverse cultural influences. From traditional Indonesian dishes to international cuisine, there is something for everyone. Be sure to try some of the local specialties, such as nasi goreng (fried rice) and satay (grilled meat skewers), which are sure to tantalize your taste buds.

When it comes to accommodation, Bali offers a wide range of options to suit all budgets and preferences. From luxury villas and five-star hotels to budget-friendly guesthouses and hostels, there is something for every traveler. Many of the accommodations are set against stunning natural backdrops, offering an unparalleled experience of island living.

Bali is a beautiful island that has something for everyone. Whether you want to relax on the beach, explore the local culture, or enjoy some adventure, Bali has it all. So, welcome to Bali, and enjoy your stay on this magical island!

Introduction

Bali is an Indonesian island province situated between Java and Lombok. It is one of the most popular tourist destinations in the world, renowned for its pristine beaches, rich cultural heritage, stunning landscapes, and warm hospitality. Bali is often referred to as the Island of the Gods, and with good reason. It is home to thousands of Hindu temples and shrines, and the local people are deeply religious and practice their faith with great fervor.

The island covers an area of 5,780 square kilometers and is home to over 4 million people. The Balinese people are known for their creativity, artistic talent, and deep respect for their cultural heritage. Their traditions and way of life are deeply intertwined with their beliefs, and this can be seen in everything from their architecture to their cuisine.

Bali's climate is tropical, with two distinct seasons: the dry season (May-September) and the rainy season (October-April). The temperature ranges from 25 to 35 degrees Celsius throughout the year, making it an ideal destination for travelers seeking a warm and sunny getaway.

The island is divided into several regions, each with its own unique character and attractions. The most popular destinations include:

Ubud: This cultural hub is famous for its art galleries, museums, and traditional dances. Visitors can also explore the stunning rice terraces and lush forests that surround the town.

Kuta: This lively beach town is popular with young travelers and surfers. It is known for its nightlife, shopping, and water sports.

Seminyak: This upscale area is home to some of the island's best restaurants, bars, and boutiques. It is also famous for its high-end spas and beach clubs.

Nusa Dua: This luxurious resort area is home to some of Bali's most exclusive hotels and beaches. It is a popular destination for honeymooners and families seeking a tranquil and luxurious getaway.

Jimbaran: This fishing village is famous for its seafood restaurants and stunning sunsets. Visitors can also enjoy a variety of water sports and beach activities.

Bali is also renowned for its stunning natural beauty. The island is home to several volcanoes, including Mount Agung, the highest point on the island. Visitors can also explore the stunning rice terraces, waterfalls, and forests that cover much of the island's interior. Bali is also surrounded by coral reefs, making it a popular destination for diving and snorkeling.

The Balinese people are renowned for their warm hospitality and friendliness. Visitors can experience this firsthand by staying in one of the island's many homestays or guesthouses. These accommodations offer an authentic glimpse into Balinese life, and guests can learn about the local culture and traditions from their hosts.

Bali's cuisine is also a highlight for many visitors. The island's cuisine is a blend of Indonesian, Chinese, and Indian influences, and is known for its use of fresh ingredients and bold flavors. Some of the must-try dishes include Nasi Goreng (fried rice), Satay (grilled meat skewers), and Babi Guling (roast suckling pig).

In addition to its natural beauty, cultural heritage, and warm hospitality, Bali is also a shopper's paradise. Visitors can explore the island's many markets and boutiques, where they can find everything from traditional handicrafts to designer clothing and accessories. Some of the most popular shopping destinations include Ubud Market, Kuta Square, and Seminyak Village.

Bali is a destination that truly has something for everyone. Whether you're seeking a relaxing beach vacation, an adventure-filled getaway, or a cultural immersion experience, Bali has it all. With its stunning natural beauty, rich cultural heritage, and warm hospitality, Bali is a destination that should be on every traveler's bucket list.

Chapter 1: "The Ultimate Bali Travel Guide: 5 Things You Need to Know Before You Go"

Best time to visit Bali

Bali is a breathtakingly beautiful Indonesian island that is often referred to as the "Island of the Gods." It is an ideal destination for tourists seeking an exotic and luxurious vacation with stunning beaches, breathtaking landscapes, delicious cuisine, rich culture, and warm hospitality. However, choosing the best time to visit Bali can be a bit tricky, as the island experiences two distinct seasons with varying weather patterns, crowds, and prices. In this article, we'll take a closer look at the different seasons in Bali and help you determine the best time to visit based on your preferences.

The two seasons in Bali are the dry season and the wet season. The dry season, which runs from May to September, is considered the best time to visit Bali, as the weather is warm, sunny, and dry, making it ideal for outdoor activities such as sunbathing, surfing, snorkeling, and diving. During this time, the island experiences low humidity and cool breezes, which make it pleasant for sightseeing and exploring the island's many temples, museums, and other attractions.

The wet season, on the other hand, runs from October to April and is characterized by frequent rainfall, high humidity, and occasional storms. While the wet season may not be the best time for sunbathing and outdoor activities, it has its own unique charm, such as lush green landscapes, fewer crowds, and lower prices on accommodation and activities. The rainy season also presents an opportunity to explore Bali's rich culture, such as traditional dances, ceremonies, and festivals that take place during this time.

If you are a surf enthusiast, the best time to visit Bali is during the dry season, as the island's south and southwest coasts experience consistent waves, making it an ideal destination for surfers. The peak surfing season is from May to September when the swell is at its best, and the famous surf spots such as Uluwatu, Padang-Padang, and Bingin are at their busiest.

If you're looking to avoid the crowds and enjoy lower prices on accommodation and activities, the wet season may be the best time to visit Bali. The period between October and November is considered the shoulder season, and it offers a good balance between the two seasons, with fewer tourists, lower prices, and fewer rainy days

Entry requirements for Bali

Passport Requirements:

All travelers to Bali must have a valid passport that is valid for at least six months beyond the date of entry. Your passport should have at least one blank page for the visa stamp. It's important to ensure that your passport is in good condition and not damaged; otherwise, you may be denied entry into Bali.

Visa Requirements:

Indonesia has a visa-free policy that allows nationals from 169 countries to enter Indonesia without a visa for up to 30 days. However, this policy only applies to tourism purposes, and visitors are not allowed to engage in any form of paid work during their stay.

If you are not eligible for a visa-free entry, you may need to apply for a visa beforehand. You can apply for a visa at an Indonesian embassy or consulate in your country or apply for a visa on arrival at Bali's Ngurah Rai International Airport. The visa on arrival is valid for 30 days and can be extended for another 30 days.

COVID-19 Requirements:

Due to the ongoing COVID-19 pandemic, Indonesia has implemented several measures to control the spread of the virus. All travelers to Bali are required to present a negative COVID-19 test result obtained within 72 hours before departure. The test must be a PCR test, and the result must be in English.

Travelers must also complete a health declaration form and undergo a health screening upon arrival at the airport. If you exhibit any COVID-19 symptoms or have been in close contact with a COVID-19 positive person, you may be subject to further testing and quarantine.

Other Requirements:

It's important to note that Bali has strict drug laws, and any possession, use, or trafficking of drugs can result in severe penalties, including imprisonment and the death penalty.

Additionally, travelers must have proof of onward travel, such as a return flight or a ticket to a third country. If you plan to stay in Bali for an extended period, you may be required to provide proof of sufficient funds to cover your stay.

To enter Bali as a tourist, you need a valid passport, a negative COVID-19 test result, and proof of onward travel. You may also need a visa, depending on your nationality. It's essential to check the entry requirements before you travel to ensure that you have all the necessary documents and meet all the criteria for entry.

Currency and exchange rates in Bali

The official currency in Bali is the Indonesian Rupiah (IDR), which is abbreviated as Rp. The exchange rate of the IDR fluctuates regularly, so it's important to check the latest rates before exchanging money.

As of my knowledge cutoff date of September 2021, the exchange rate for 1 USD was approximately 14,425 IDR. However, exchange rates can vary depending on where you exchange your money and what time of day it is. It's always a good idea to compare exchange rates at different exchange booths or banks before making a transaction to ensure you get the best deal.

When it comes to exchanging currency in Bali, there are several options available to travelers. One of the most convenient ways to exchange money is to withdraw cash from an ATM. ATMs are readily available throughout Bali, especially in popular tourist areas such as Kuta, Seminyak, and Ubud. However, it's important to note that some ATMs charge fees for withdrawals, and some may have lower withdrawal limits than what you're used to in your home country.

Another option for exchanging currency in Bali is to use a money changer. Money changers can be found all over the island, especially in tourist areas. It's important to choose a reputable money changer that is licensed by the Indonesian Central Bank (BI). Be sure to count your money carefully before leaving the booth, and check for any hidden fees or unfavorable exchange rates.

Credit cards are also widely accepted in Bali, especially at larger establishments such as hotels and restaurants. However, smaller businesses and market vendors may only accept cash. It's always a good idea to have a mix of cash and cards on hand when traveling in Bali.

Finally, it's important to note that Bali is a popular tourist destination, and some businesses may try to take advantage of tourists by offering unfavorable exchange rates or adding hidden fees. Always do your research before exchanging money or making purchases, and be aware of any scams or frauds that may be common in the area.

Travelers to Bali should be aware of the official currency (Indonesian Rupiah) and the current exchange rates. It's important to compare rates at different exchange booths or banks to ensure you get the best deal. ATMs, money changers, and credit cards are all viable options for exchanging money in Bali, but it's important to exercise caution and do your research to avoid scams and unfavorable rates

Language and culture in Bali

As a traveler to Bali, understanding the language and culture can greatly enhance your experience on the island. Here's a long note on language and culture in Bali for travelers to Bali.

Language in Bali:

The official language of Bali is Indonesian, which is widely spoken throughout the island. However, the Balinese people have their own language, which is also called Balinese. Balinese is part of the Austronesian language family and is closely related to other languages spoken in Indonesia, such as Javanese and Sundanese.

Although Indonesian is the official language of Bali, many Balinese people still use Balinese in their everyday lives, particularly in rural areas. If you are traveling to Bali, it is helpful to learn a few common phrases in Balinese, such as greetings, thank you, and please. Learning a few words in the local language can show respect for the local culture and help you connect with the people you meet.

Culture in Bali:

The Balinese culture is a unique blend of Hinduism and local traditions. Balinese Hinduism is different from Hinduism practiced in India, with unique beliefs, rituals, and festivals. The Balinese people are known for their hospitality and friendliness, making it easy for travelers to connect with them.

Cultural practices to keep in mind when traveling to Bali:

Dress modestly: Bali is a conservative culture, so it is important to dress modestly, particularly when visiting temples or other religious sites. Both men and women should cover their shoulders and knees, and women should avoid wearing revealing clothing.

Respect local customs: The Balinese people have their own customs and traditions, and it is important to respect them. For example, it is customary to remove your shoes before entering someone's home or a temple.

Learn about the local festivals: Bali is known for its colorful festivals, which are an important part of the culture. If you are traveling to Bali during a festival, such as Galungan or Nyepi, take the time to learn about the customs and participate in the festivities.

Greet people with a smile: The Balinese people are known for their friendly and welcoming nature. When you meet someone, greet them with a smile and show interest in their culture and traditions.

Participate in local activities: Bali is home to many unique activities, such as traditional dance performances, cooking classes, and handicraft workshops. Participating in these activities can help you gain a deeper understanding of the local culture and connect with the people you meet.

Bali is a unique and fascinating destination that offers a rich cultural experience for travelers. Learning a few words in the local language and respecting local customs can greatly enhance your experience on the island. By immersing yourself in the local culture, you can gain a deeper appreciation for the Balinese people and their way of life

Safety tips for traveling to Bali

As with any travel destination, it is important to take certain safety precautions to ensure a safe and enjoyable trip. Some safety tips to consider when traveling to Bali:

Tips1: Stay aware of your surroundings
One of the most important things to do when traveling to Bali is to stay aware of your surroundings. Bali is generally a safe destination, but like anywhere, there is a risk of

theft, pickpocketing, and other crimes. Be aware of your surroundings, especially in crowded areas such as markets, beaches, and tourist attractions. Keep an eye on your belongings and avoid carrying large amounts of cash or valuables.

Tips2: Be cautious of traffic
Bali's roads can be chaotic and congested, especially in busy areas like Kuta, Seminyak, and Denpasar. If you plan on renting a motorbike or scooter, make sure you are comfortable with driving in Bali's traffic. Wear a helmet at all times and be aware of other drivers on the road. If you are not comfortable with driving a motorbike or scooter, consider hiring a driver or taking a taxi.

Tips3: Stay hydrated
Bali's climate is tropical, with hot and humid temperatures year-round. It is important to stay hydrated to avoid heat exhaustion and dehydration. Drink plenty of water throughout

the day and avoid alcohol and caffeine, which can dehydrate you even more. If you are planning on spending time in the sun, wear a hat, sunglasses, and sunscreen to protect yourself from the sun's harmful rays.

Tips4: Avoid drugs
Drug laws in Bali are strict, and possession of even small amounts of drugs can lead to severe penalties, including lengthy prison sentences and even the death penalty. Do not accept drugs from strangers, and do not purchase or use drugs while in Bali. Police often conduct random drug tests, and tourists who test positive for drugs face legal consequences.

Tips 5: Watch out for scams
Tourist scams are common in Bali, and it is important to be aware of them to avoid being a victim. Common scams include taxi drivers overcharging for rides, fake tour companies, and people posing as police officers asking for bribes. Be cautious of people who approach you

offering tours or services, and only use reputable tour companies or taxi services.

Tips 6: Respect local customs and traditions
Bali is known for its unique culture and customs, and it is important to respect them while visiting the island. Dress modestly when visiting temples or other religious sites, and remove your shoes before entering. Be respectful of local customs, and avoid making derogatory comments or gestures towards locals or their customs.

Tips 7: Stay safe in the water
Bali is a popular destination for water activities, including surfing, snorkeling, and diving. However, it is important to stay safe while in the water. Always swim in areas that are supervised by lifeguards, and be aware of strong currents and rip tides. If you are not a strong swimmer, consider taking a swimming lesson or hiring a guide to accompany you.

Tips 8: Keep important documents safe

Make copies of your passport, visa, and other important documents and keep them in a safe place. Consider using a money belt or pouch to keep your documents and valuables close to your body. If you are staying in a hotel or villa, use the safe room to store your passport and other valuables.

Tips 9: Get travel insurance
It is important to have travel insurance when traveling to Bali, as accidents and illnesses can happen. Make sure your travel insurance covers medical expenses, as well as emergency medical evacuation in case of a serious injury or illness. If you plan on participating in adventure sports or activities, make sure your insurance covers these activities

Chapter 2: "Discover Bali: 5 Must-Visit Places on Your Trip"

Ubud: Cultural Heart of Bali

Ubud, located in the heart of Bali, is a must-visit destination for travelers seeking to immerse themselves in Balinese culture. With its lush green landscapes, rich cultural heritage, and vibrant artistic community, Ubud has become a cultural hub and an epicenter for all things art and tradition.

Ubud has a rich cultural history dating back centuries. The town is home to numerous ancient temples, palaces, and shrines that are still in use today. The most famous of these is the Pura Taman Saraswati temple, which is located in the center of town and features a stunning lotus pond that is surrounded by beautiful traditional Balinese architecture.

One of the main draws of Ubud is its thriving art scene. The town is home to countless art galleries, museums, and workshops, making it a perfect destination for anyone interested in traditional Balinese art, from wood carvings and batik textiles to traditional dances and gamelan music. Ubud is also known for its thriving creative community, with many artists, writers, and musicians calling it home.

Beyond the arts, Ubud is also a great place to explore Bali's natural beauty. The town is surrounded by lush rice paddies and jungles, and there are many opportunities for hiking and outdoor adventures. The nearby Monkey Forest Sanctuary is a must-visit, as it offers visitors a chance to see the playful monkeys that inhabit the area up close.

One of the best ways to experience Ubud is to take part in one of its many cultural events and festivals. The town is known for its vibrant and colorful festivals, such as the Ubud Writers and Readers Festival, the Bali Spirit Festival, and the

Ubud Food Festival. These events offer visitors a chance to connect with locals, experience traditional Balinese culture, and enjoy live music and performances.

Ubud is also known for its wellness offerings, with many yoga studios, spas, and retreats catering to travelers seeking relaxation and rejuvenation. From traditional Balinese massages to meditation and yoga classes, Ubud has something for everyone looking to unwind and recharge.

In all Ubud is a must-visit destination for anyone looking to experience Balinese culture, art, and tradition. With its vibrant arts scene, beautiful natural surroundings, and rich cultural heritage, Ubud offers a unique and unforgettable travel experience.

Kuta, the surfing paradise

Kuta is a vibrant and bustling beach town located on the southern coast of Bali, Indonesia. Known for its spectacular beaches and world-class surfing waves, Kuta is a must-visit destination for anyone looking to experience the best that Bali has to offer.

One of the main attractions in Kuta is its incredible surfing conditions. The beach is renowned for its consistent and challenging waves, making it a popular spot for surfers of all skill levels. Beginners can take lessons from experienced instructors, while more experienced surfers can tackle the larger waves further out to sea. Kuta Beach is also home to some of the best surf schools in Bali, with certified instructors and quality equipment available for rent.

Aside from surfing, Kuta offers a wide range of activities and attractions for travelers of all ages and interests. Visitors can explore the vibrant local markets, sample delicious local cuisine, or relax on the beach and soak up the sun. There are also plenty of opportunities for water sports, such as jet skiing, parasailing, and scuba diving.

One of the most iconic attractions in Kuta is the Kuta Beachwalk, a modern shopping mall with a range of high-end boutiques, restaurants, and entertainment options. Here, visitors can enjoy a day of shopping and dining in a beautiful oceanfront setting.

For those interested in Balinese culture, Kuta offers a range of cultural experiences and attractions. The Bali Bombing Memorial, located on the site of the 2002 terrorist attack that killed over 200 people, is a somber yet important reminder of Bali's history and resilience. Visitors can also visit the nearby Pura Tanah Lot temple, one of Bali's most iconic and picturesque temples, located on a stunning clifftop overlooking the ocean.

In terms of accommodation, Kuta offers a wide range of options to suit all budgets and preferences. From luxurious beachfront resorts to budget-friendly guesthouses, there are plenty of options available for travelers of all types.

Overall, Kuta is a must-visit destination for anyone traveling to Bali. With its incredible surfing conditions, stunning beaches, vibrant culture, and range of activities and attractions, Kuta truly has something for everyone. Whether you're a seasoned surfer, a culture enthusiast, or simply looking to relax and soak up the sun, Kuta is a destination that should not be missed.

Seminyak, the trendy beach town

Seminyak is a trendy and chic beach town located on the southwestern coast of Bali, Indonesia. It is renowned for its upscale resorts, high-end spas, and luxurious villas. The town's stunning beaches, lively nightlife, world-class restaurants, and fashionable boutiques make it one of the most sought-after destinations in Bali.

One of the main attractions of Seminyak is its beautiful beaches, including Seminyak Beach, Petitenget Beach, and Batu Belig Beach. These beaches offer visitors an opportunity to relax and enjoy the sun, sand, and surf. Seminyak Beach is particularly popular for its stunning sunsets, which attract visitors from all over the world.

Seminyak is also a great destination for those looking to experience Bali's unique culture. The town is home to several temples, including the famous Pura Petitenget, which dates back to the 16th century. Visitors can witness traditional Balinese ceremonies and rituals at these temples, providing a fascinating insight into the island's rich cultural heritage.

Seminyak is also renowned for its dining scene, with some of Bali's best restaurants located here. The town's dining options range from traditional Balinese cuisine to international flavors, including Japanese, Italian, and Mexican. Some of the popular restaurants in Seminyak include Ku De Ta, Sarong, and Metis.

For those looking to indulge in some retail therapy, Seminyak is a paradise. The town is home to a range of fashionable boutiques, selling everything from designer clothing and accessories to local handicrafts. Some of the popular shopping destinations in Seminyak include Seminyak Square, Seminyak Village, and Oberoi Street.

Seminyak's nightlife is also a major draw for visitors. The town is home to several bars, clubs, and lounges, providing a vibrant and lively atmosphere after dark. Some of the popular nightlife spots in Seminyak include Potato Head Beach Club, La Favela, and Red Carpet Champagne Bar.

Accommodation options in Seminyak are plentiful, ranging from budget-friendly guesthouses to luxury resorts and villas. Some of the popular resorts in Seminyak include The

Legian Bali, The Oberoi Bali, and W Bali – Seminyak.

Finally, Seminyak is a must-visit destination for anyone traveling to Bali. Its beautiful beaches, rich culture, world-class dining and shopping, and vibrant nightlife make it an ideal destination for those seeking a luxurious and unforgettable experience.

Nusa Penida, the island paradise

Nusa Penida is an island paradise located in the southeastern part of Bali, Indonesia. It is a relatively untouched island that offers a unique and authentic experience to travelers who want to escape the crowds and explore the beauty of Bali's hidden gem. The island is famous for its pristine beaches, crystal clear waters, stunning cliffs, and rich marine life, making it a must-visit destination for travelers who love nature and adventure.

Getting to Nusa Penida is easy. It can be accessed by a fast boat from Sanur or Padang Bai harbor in Bali, and the journey takes around 30-45 minutes. Once on the island, travelers can explore the island's various attractions, including the famous Kelingking Beach, Angel's Billabong, Broken Beach, Crystal Bay, and Atuh Beach. These attractions are popular for their breathtaking views, white sandy beaches, and crystal clear waters that are perfect for swimming, snorkeling, and diving.

One of the island's most popular attractions is Kelingking Beach, also known as T-Rex Beach, which is located on the western coast of the island. The beach is famous for its unique rock formation that resembles a T-Rex dinosaur, and the panoramic views of the ocean from the top of the cliff. Visitors can trek down the steep path to reach the beach and enjoy the crystal clear waters and white sandy beaches.

Another popular attraction on the island is Angel's Billabong, a natural infinity pool that is formed by the ocean's waves crashing against the rocks. The clear blue water, surrounded by the lush greenery of the island, offers a stunning view and a perfect spot for swimming and relaxing.

Broken Beach, located nearby to Angel's Billabong, is another natural wonder of the island, where a natural archway has formed over the years by the ocean waves, creating a beautiful lagoon that is only accessible from the top of the cliffs. The views from the top of the cliffs are breathtaking, and the blue waters of the lagoon are perfect for swimming and snorkeling.

Crystal Bay, located on the western coast of the island, is a beautiful beach famous for its crystal clear waters and coral reefs. It is one of the best spots for snorkeling and diving on the island, where visitors can explore the rich marine life of the island, including colorful fish, sea turtles, and even manta rays.

Atuh Beach, located on the eastern coast of the island, is a beautiful hidden gem that offers stunning views of the ocean and the surrounding cliffs. It is a perfect spot for swimming, sunbathing, and relaxing on the white sandy beach.

Apart from the beautiful beaches and stunning landscapes, Nusa Penida also offers cultural experiences to visitors. Visitors can visit the island's traditional villages and temples to learn about the island's history and culture. The island's main religion is Hinduism, and visitors can witness colorful ceremonies and rituals that are performed by the locals.

Nusa Penida is a must-visit destination for travelers who love nature, adventure, and culture. The island's pristine beaches, crystal clear waters, stunning cliffs, and rich marine life offer a unique and authentic experience to visitors who want to escape the crowds and explore Bali's hidden gem. It is an ideal destination for those who seek tranquility, adventure, and beauty in their travels.

Tanah Lot Temple, the iconic Bali landmark

Tanah Lot Temple is an iconic landmark and one of the most popular tourist attractions on the island of Bali, Indonesia. Located on the southwestern coast of Bali, the temple is built on a rocky outcrop that stands just offshore, surrounded by the Indian Ocean. Tanah Lot is an important cultural and spiritual site for the Balinese people, and visitors come from all over the world to experience its stunning beauty and unique atmosphere.

The temple itself dates back to the 16th century and is dedicated to the sea gods. It is one of seven sea temples along the Balinese coast and is believed to have been founded by a Javanese priest named Dang Hyang Nirartha. According to legend, Nirartha saw the rock formation off the coast and decided to build a temple there to honor the sea gods. Today, Tanah Lot is still an active temple, and visitors can witness daily offerings and ceremonies.

One of the reasons why Tanah Lot is so popular is its stunning natural setting. The temple is perched on top of a large rock that juts out into the ocean, and at high tide, the waves crash against the base of the rock, creating a dramatic and unforgettable scene. As the sun sets over the Indian Ocean, the temple is bathed in a golden glow, making for a truly magical experience.

Visitors can access Tanah Lot via a short walk from the parking area, and there are numerous vendors selling souvenirs and snacks along the way. The temple is open to the public from 7 am to 7 pm, and admission fees apply. It is advisable to arrive early in the day to avoid the crowds and to take advantage of the cooler temperatures.

In addition to the temple itself, there are a number of other attractions to explore in the surrounding area. The nearby town of Tabanan is known for its beautiful rice terraces, and visitors can also take a stroll through the nearby Tanah Lot Cultural Park, which features a variety of traditional Balinese architecture and artwork. For those interested in water sports, there are several surfing spots along the coast, and the nearby Nirwana Bali Golf Club is a popular destination for golfers.

Overall, Tanah Lot Temple is a must-visit destination for anyone traveling to Bali. Its stunning natural beauty, rich cultural history, and unique atmosphere make it an unforgettable experience for visitors of all ages. Whether you're looking to explore Bali's spiritual side, witness a beautiful sunset, or simply take in the breathtaking scenery, Tanah Lot is sure to impress.

Chapter 3: "Bali on a Budget: 5 Tips for Traveling to Bali on a Shoestring"

Affordable accommodations in Bali

For travelers on a budget, finding affordable accommodations in Bali can be a challenge. However, there are plenty of options available that can make your trip to Bali both enjoyable and affordable.

One of the most popular options for affordable accommodations in Bali is to stay in a guesthouse or homestay. These are usually small, family-run businesses that offer comfortable rooms at a reasonable price. Many guesthouses and homestays are located in traditional Balinese villages, giving travelers an authentic experience of Balinese culture and way of life.

Another popular option for affordable accommodations in Bali is to stay in a hostel. Hostels in Bali offer dormitory-style rooms, which are ideal for solo travelers or groups of friends traveling together. Hostels are also a great way to meet other travelers and make new friends.

For those who want a bit more privacy, there are also plenty of budget hotels and guesthouses in Bali that offer comfortable rooms at a reasonable price. These hotels may not have the luxury amenities of more expensive resorts, but they provide a clean and comfortable place to stay while exploring the island.

If you're looking for a more unique and adventurous experience, you can also consider staying in a treehouse or bamboo hut. These types of accommodations are becoming increasingly popular in Bali, and they offer a one-of-a-kind experience that you won't find anywhere else.

Finally, if you're willing to do a bit of research and planning, you can also find great deals on vacation rentals in Bali. Websites like Airbnb and VRBO offer a wide range of affordable accommodations, including villas, apartments, and houses, that can be rented for a fraction of the cost of a traditional hotel.

There are plenty of affordable accommodations in Bali for travelers on a budget. Whether you're looking for a guesthouse, hostel, budget hotel, treehouse, or vacation rental, there are plenty of options available that can help you make the most of your trip to this beautiful island. So start planning your Bali adventure today and discover all that this amazing destination has to offer!

Cheap eats in Bali

Bali, Indonesia is a popular travel destination known for its stunning beaches, lush rice terraces, rich culture, and delicious food. While there are plenty of high-end restaurants and luxury dining options available in Bali, there are also a variety of cheap eats that offer great value for budget-conscious travelers. In this note, we will explore some of the best cheap eats in Bali for travelers on a budget.

Warungs:
Warungs are small, family-owned restaurants that serve traditional Indonesian cuisine at affordable prices. These eateries are found throughout Bali, and they are a great option for budget travelers who want to sample authentic Indonesian dishes without breaking the bank. Some popular warungs in Bali include Warung Sopa in Ubud, Warung Babi Guling Pak Dobiel in Seminyak, and Warung Mak Beng in Sanur.

Street Food: Bali is home to a vibrant street food scene, with food vendors selling a wide range of dishes on the side of the road or in night markets. Some popular street food options include satay (skewered meat), nasi goreng (fried rice), and gado-gado (vegetable salad with peanut sauce). The best places to find street food in Bali are in Denpasar, Kuta, and Seminyak.

Local Markets: Bali is home to a variety of local markets where visitors can find fresh produce, spices, and street food. Some of the most popular markets in Bali include Pasar Badung in Denpasar, Ubud Market in Ubud, and Kumbasari Market in Sanur. These markets are a great place to sample local delicacies and experience the vibrant culture of Bali.

Cafes: Bali is home to a variety of trendy cafes that serve delicious food and drinks at affordable prices. Many of these cafes also offer free Wi-Fi, making them a great place for budget travelers to relax and catch up on work. Some popular cafes in Bali include Revolver Espresso in Seminyak, Betelnut Cafe in Canggu, and Cafe Organic in Seminyak.

Warung-style Buffets: Some warungs offer buffet-style meals where customers can sample a variety of dishes at an affordable price. This is a great option for budget travelers who want to try a variety of Indonesian dishes without spending a lot of money. Some popular warung-style buffets in Bali include Warung Wardani in Denpasar and Warung Nasi Ayam Bu Oki in Seminyak.

Bali offers a variety of cheap eats for budget-conscious travelers. Whether you're looking for traditional Indonesian cuisine at a warung, street food in a night market, or a trendy cafe with free Wi-Fi, Bali has something to offer. By exploring the local food scene, visitors to Bali can experience the culture and flavors of this beautiful island without spending a lot of money.

Free or low-cost activities in Bali

Here are some of the best free or low-cost activities to do in Bali:

Beaches: Bali is known for its stunning beaches, and many of them are free to access. Kuta Beach, Seminyak Beach, and Sanur Beach are some of the most popular and easily accessible beaches. While some beaches may charge for sun loungers or umbrellas, many travelers simply bring a towel and enjoy the sand and surf.

Temples: Bali is also known for its beautiful Hindu temples, many of which are free to visit. Tanah Lot, Uluwatu, and Tirta Empul are just a few of the temples that travelers can explore. It's important to dress respectfully when visiting temples, as they are considered sacred places.

Rice Terraces: Bali's famous rice terraces are a must-see for travelers. The Tegalalang Rice

Terrace is one of the most popular and accessible rice terraces, with stunning views of the rice paddies and surrounding landscape. There may be a small fee for parking or entrance, but it's generally very affordable.

Waterfalls: Bali is home to some stunning waterfalls, many of which are free to visit. Some of the most popular waterfalls include Tegenungan Waterfall, Gitgit Waterfall, and Sekumpul Waterfall. Visitors should be prepared for some hiking and walking to reach some of the waterfalls.

Markets: Bali's markets are a great place to experience local culture and pick up souvenirs. The Ubud Art Market, Sukawati Market, and Kuta Art Market are just a few of the markets that travelers can explore. Be prepared to haggle for the best prices!

Cultural Performances: Bali is known for its traditional dance and music performances, many of which are free to watch. Some of the best places to see cultural performances include the Ubud Palace, Pura Dalem Temple, and Taman Budaya Cultural Center.

Hiking and Trekking: Bali's landscape is perfect for hiking and trekking, and there are many trails that are free to explore. Mount Batur is a popular destination for hiking, with stunning views of the sunrise from the summit. Other popular hiking destinations include Mount Agung, Mount Abang, and Campuhan Ridge Walk.

Museums: Bali has a rich cultural history, and there are many museums that travelers can visit to learn more about Balinese culture. The Museum Puri Lukisan, Agung Rai Museum of Art, and Neka Art Museum are just a few of the museums that travelers can explore.

How to negotiate prices in Bali

Do Your Research: Before you start negotiating, do some research on the items you want to buy. Find out the average price of the item in the market and what other vendors are charging for it. This will give you an idea of how much you should be paying and will help you avoid being ripped off.

Be Polite and Friendly: Politeness and friendliness can go a long way when negotiating prices. Smile and greet the vendor, engage in small talk, and show genuine interest in their products. This can create a positive atmosphere and make the vendor more willing to negotiate.

Start with a Low Price: When negotiating, it's always a good idea to start with a low price. This gives you room to negotiate and also shows the vendor that you know the value of the item. However, don't go too low, as this can be seen as disrespectful and can offend the vendor.

Counter Offer: The vendor may offer a price higher than what you are willing to pay. In this case, counter with a price that is slightly lower than what you are willing to pay. This shows the vendor that you are willing to negotiate and can lead to a fair price for both parties.

Stick to Your Budget: It's important to have a budget in mind before you start negotiating. Stick to your budget and don't let the vendor pressure you into paying more than you can afford. If the vendor isn't willing to meet your price, it's okay to walk away.

Bundle Your Purchases: If you're buying multiple items from the same vendor, try bundling them together and negotiating a lower price for the entire package. This can be an effective way to save money and get a good deal.

Don't Be Afraid to Walk Away: If you're not happy with the price or the vendor is being unreasonable, don't be afraid to walk away.

There are plenty of other vendors selling the same items, and you may find a better deal elsewhere.

Finally, negotiating prices in Bali can be a fun and rewarding experience for travelers. By doing your research, being polite and friendly, starting with a low price, counter offering, sticking to your budget, bundling your purchases, and not being afraid to walk away, you can negotiate a fair price and get a good deal on your purchases. Just remember to be respectful and enjoy the experience!

Budget-friendly transportation options in Bali

Bali, the Island of Gods, is a popular tourist destination with an abundance of stunning beaches, lush green rice terraces, vibrant culture, and mouth-watering cuisine. However, getting around Bali can be a bit of a challenge for travelers on a budget. Here are some budget-friendly transportation options for travelers to Bali:

Motorbike Rental: Renting a motorbike is a popular and cost-effective way to explore Bali. It is easy to find motorbike rental shops all over Bali, and rental rates are affordable. Most rental shops offer daily, weekly, or monthly rentals, and rates can range from IDR 50,000 to IDR 150,000 per day, depending on the type of motorbike and the duration of the rental. However, keep in mind that traffic in Bali can be chaotic, and driving a motorbike in Bali requires some skill and experience.

Bicycle Rental: For those who prefer a slower pace, renting a bicycle is a great option. Many guesthouses and hotels offer bicycle rentals, and rates are usually around IDR 30,000 to IDR 50,000 per day. Cycling around Bali is a great way to explore the island's picturesque countryside, and it is also a great way to get some exercise.

Public Transportation: Bali has a public transportation system, which includes buses, minivans, and bemos (small shared taxis). However, the public transportation system can be confusing for travelers who are not familiar with the routes and schedules. Buses and minivans are usually the cheapest option, with fares ranging from IDR 5,000 to IDR 20,000 depending on the distance traveled. Bemos are slightly more expensive, with fares ranging from IDR 10,000 to IDR 30,000.

Ride-Hailing Services: Ride-hailing services such as Gojek and Grab are widely available in Bali, and they offer a convenient and affordable way to get around the island. Ride-hailing fares in Bali are generally cheaper than traditional taxis, and they can be ordered using a smartphone app. However, keep in mind that some areas in Bali have restrictions on ride-hailing services, so it is important to check before using these services.

Traditional Taxis: Traditional taxis are available in Bali, but they tend to be more expensive than other transportation options. Taxi fares in Bali are usually metered, but it is important to make sure that the driver uses the meter and that the fare is agreed upon before starting the journey.

Bali offers a variety of budget-friendly transportation options for travelers. From motorbike rentals to public transportation, there is something for everyone. It is important to choose the transportation option that best suits your needs and budget, and to always negotiate prices before starting the journey. With a little bit of planning, getting around Bali can be easy and affordable.

Chapter 4: "The Ultimate Foodie's Guide to Bali: 5 Must-Try Dishes"

Nasi Goreng, the national dish of Indonesia

Nasi Goreng is a popular dish that originates from Indonesia, and it is considered the national dish of the country. This dish is a must-try when visiting Bali, which is one of the most popular tourist destinations in Indonesia. Nasi Goreng is a versatile dish, and there are many variations of it. However, the essential ingredients include rice, vegetables, meat, and a blend of spices.

The name Nasi Goreng means "fried rice" in Indonesian, and it is a staple dish in Indonesian cuisine. The dish consists of cooked rice that is stir-fried with a variety of ingredients, including vegetables, meat, seafood, and spices. The vegetables commonly used in Nasi Goreng include onions, garlic, carrots, and peas. The meat used can be chicken, beef, or pork. However, it is not uncommon to find variations of the dish that use seafood or tofu instead of meat.

The spices used in Nasi Goreng are what give the dish its unique flavor. The most commonly used spices include chili, coriander, cumin, and turmeric. These spices give the dish a spicy and aromatic flavor that is characteristic of Indonesian cuisine.

One of the best places to try Nasi Goreng in Bali is at a local warung, which is a small, family-owned restaurant that serves traditional Indonesian cuisine. These warungs are found all over Bali, and they offer a variety of dishes at affordable prices.

When ordering Nasi Goreng in Bali, there are a few things to keep in mind. First, the level of spiciness can vary, so it is essential to let the server know how spicy you want your dish to be. Second, the dish is often served with a fried egg on top, which adds an extra layer of flavor to the dish.

Overall, Nasi Goreng is a delicious and versatile dish that is a must-try when visiting Bali. Whether you prefer it with meat or seafood, spicy or mild, Nasi Goreng is a dish that will leave you wanting more. So, be sure to add it to your list of must-eat dishes when visiting Bali, and you won't be disappointed!

Babi Guling, Bali's famous suckling pig

Babi Guling, or suckling pig, is a traditional Balinese dish that is widely regarded as one of the must-eat dishes in Bali. It is a dish that is steeped in tradition and has been a part of Balinese culture for centuries. Babi Guling is so beloved in Bali that it is served at many ceremonies, such as weddings and religious celebrations.

The dish itself is made from a young pig that is roasted on a spit until it is crispy and golden brown. The pig is typically seasoned with a blend of spices that includes turmeric, coriander, lemongrass, and other local herbs and spices. The result is a tender and flavorful meat that is juicy on the inside and crispy on the outside.

Babi Guling is traditionally served with a variety of accompaniments, including steamed rice, vegetables, and sambal. Sambal is a chili-based condiment that is used to add spice and flavor to the dish. Other accompaniments may include crispy pork skin, fried shallots, and coconut milk.

The preparation of Babi Guling is a labor-intensive process that requires a great deal of skill and attention to detail. The pig is typically cooked on a spit over an open flame for several hours, and it must be turned regularly to ensure that it is cooked evenly. The seasoning of the pig is also critical, as the right blend of spices can elevate the dish from good to great.

While Babi Guling is a traditional Balinese dish, it has gained widespread popularity among tourists in recent years. Many restaurants and street vendors now offer Babi Guling as a menu item, and it is considered one of the must-try dishes in Bali. Some of the most famous Babi Guling restaurants in Bali include Ibu Oka in Ubud and Warung Babi Guling Pak Dobiel in Seminyak.

Babi Guling is not only a delicious dish but also an important part of Balinese culture. The dish is often served at important ceremonies, such as weddings and religious celebrations, and it is a symbol of community and togetherness. The preparation and sharing of Babi Guling is a way to bring people together and celebrate the richness and diversity of Balinese culture.

Babi Guling is a must-try dish for anyone visiting Bali. It is a dish that is steeped in tradition and culture, and it is an excellent way to experience the flavors and spices of Balinese cuisine. Whether enjoyed at a ceremony or in a restaurant, Babi Guling is sure to leave a lasting impression on anyone who tries it.

Sate, Indonesian-style grilled meat skewers

Sate, also known as satay, is a popular Indonesian dish that consists of grilled meat skewers marinated in a mixture of spices and served with a variety of condiments. This dish is a must-try for anyone visiting Bali, where it is a ubiquitous street food found in night markets, food carts, and restaurants.

The history of sate in Indonesia can be traced back to the 19th century, when it was introduced by Javanese street vendors who sold the grilled meat skewers as a snack to their customers. Over time, sate became more popular and began to be served as a main course in restaurants, where it was often accompanied by rice and vegetables.

Today, sate is made using a variety of meats, including chicken, beef, pork, and lamb, although chicken and beef are the most popular choices. The meat is typically cut into small, bite-sized pieces and marinated in a blend of spices and herbs, including turmeric, coriander, cumin, lemongrass, and garlic. The marinated meat is then skewered and grilled over an open flame until it is cooked to perfection.

In Bali, sate is often served with a peanut sauce that is made by blending roasted peanuts with chili, garlic, sugar, and tamarind paste. The sauce is thick and creamy, with a slightly sweet and spicy flavor that compliments the smoky taste of the grilled meat. Other condiments that are commonly served with sate in Bali include sliced shallots, cucumber, and kecap manis, a sweet soy sauce that is similar to molasses.

Sate can be enjoyed as a snack or a full meal, depending on the quantity and accompaniments. In Bali, it is often served as an appetizer or a side dish at restaurants, but it is also a popular street food that is sold by vendors on carts or bicycles. Visitors to Bali can try sate at night markets like Pasar Malam or in popular restaurants like Warung Sate Bali, Sate Babi Bawah Pohon, and Sate Plecing Arjuna.

In addition to its delicious flavor, sate is also a convenient and portable food that can be eaten on the go. The skewers make it easy to hold and eat the meat without getting your hands dirty, which makes it a popular choice for outdoor events and festivals.

Overall, sate is a must-try dish for anyone visiting Bali, where it is a beloved street food that is enjoyed by locals and tourists alike.

Whether you prefer chicken, beef, or pork, there is a sate skewer for everyone, and the spicy peanut sauce and other condiments only add to the delicious flavor of this Indonesian classic.

Gado-gado, a salad of mixed vegetables and peanut sauce

Gado-gado is a popular Indonesian salad made with a mixture of vegetables and served with a flavorful peanut sauce. It is a must-try dish when visiting Bali, a popular tourist destination in Indonesia. This salad is not only delicious but also healthy, as it is packed with various nutritious vegetables.

The name "gado-gado" comes from the Indonesian word "gado," which means to mix. The salad is made by mixing different types of vegetables, such as cabbage, bean sprouts, carrots, spinach, and cucumber, along with boiled eggs and tofu. These vegetables are blanched or lightly steamed to maintain their crunchiness.

The peanut sauce is the star of the dish, as it provides a rich and nutty flavor. The sauce is made by blending roasted peanuts with garlic, shallots, chilies, and tamarind paste. The mixture is then thinned out with coconut milk, water, and sweet soy sauce to make it into a smooth and creamy consistency.

The salad is typically served with a side of shrimp crackers, which are used to scoop up the peanut sauce. It is a perfect dish for those who want a light yet satisfying meal. Gado-gado can be found in most warungs (local eateries) and restaurants in Bali, and it is usually served as a vegetarian dish. However, some versions may also include meat or seafood.

Gado-gado is not only popular in Bali but also throughout Indonesia. It is often considered a national dish and is enjoyed by people from all walks of life. The dish is also versatile, as it can be modified according to personal preferences. Some variations may include different types of vegetables, such as green beans or potatoes, while others may use different types of nuts, such as cashews or almonds.

Overall, gado-gado is a must-try dish when visiting Bali. It is a perfect representation of Indonesian cuisine, which is known for its bold and complex flavors. So, if you are looking for a healthy and delicious meal, head over to a local warung and order a plate of gado-gado with a side of shrimp crackers. You won't be disappointed!

Lawar, a traditional Balinese dish made with minced meat and spices

Lawar is a traditional Balinese dish that has become a staple in Balinese cuisine. This dish is a combination of minced meat, vegetables, and spices, and is often served with rice. Lawar is a must-try for anyone visiting Bali, as it represents the local culture and the Balinese way of life.

The main ingredient in Lawar is usually either minced pork or chicken. The meat is then mixed with freshly grated coconut, and a variety of spices such as turmeric, ginger, garlic, and chili. The dish is then further flavored with kaffir lime leaves, lemongrass, and shallots, which give it a unique aroma and flavor.

One of the key features of Lawar is the use of fresh vegetables, which are usually finely chopped and mixed into the dish. The vegetables commonly used in Lawar include long beans, bean sprouts, grated carrots, and shredded coconut. These vegetables provide a crisp texture and a fresh taste to the dish, making it even more delicious.

Lawar is typically served with steamed rice and a side of sambal, a spicy chili paste that adds an extra kick of heat to the dish. It is often enjoyed as a main course, but can also be served as a side dish or an appetizer.

One of the unique aspects of Lawar is that it is often prepared in a communal setting. In Bali, Lawar is commonly made for special occasions such as temple ceremonies or weddings, and family members and friends will gather together to prepare the dish. This communal preparation adds to the social aspect of the dish, and is a reflection of the strong sense of community and togetherness in Balinese culture.

While Lawar may not be as well-known as some of the other Indonesian dishes, it is a must-try for anyone visiting Bali. The combination of flavors and textures in this dish is truly unique, and it offers a delicious and authentic taste of Balinese cuisine. Whether enjoyed in a local warung (small restaurant), or as part of a traditional Balinese ceremony, Lawar is sure to leave a lasting impression on anyone who tries it.

Chapter 5: "Relax and Recharge: 5 Best Wellness Retreats in Bali"

COMO Shambhala Estate, Ubud

COMO Shambhala Estate is widely considered as one of the best wellness retreats in Bali, Indonesia. Located in Ubud, the heart of Bali's cultural and spiritual center, the estate offers a tranquil and serene environment for guests to unwind and rejuvenate. The estate sits on a sprawling 23-acre property that boasts a stunning landscape of verdant rice terraces, flowing rivers, and lush tropical forests.

The wellness retreat is designed to cater to the needs of guests seeking a holistic approach to health and wellbeing. COMO Shambhala Estate is renowned for its exceptional service, world-class facilities, and wellness programs that integrate ancient healing traditions with modern scientific approaches. The retreat's programs are personalized to meet the unique needs of each guest, ensuring that they leave feeling refreshed, recharged, and reconnected.

The estate offers various accommodation options, ranging from rooms and suites to private villas, each designed to provide guests with a luxurious and comfortable retreat. The rooms are beautifully decorated with contemporary Balinese furniture and feature amenities such as air conditioning, satellite TV, and high-speed Wi-Fi. The private villas, on the other hand, offer guests an unparalleled level of privacy and luxury, with features such as private pools, outdoor showers, and stunning views of the surrounding landscape.

One of the highlights of COMO Shambhala Estate is its award-winning wellness programs that cater to various aspects of health and wellbeing. The retreat's wellness programs are designed to help guests achieve optimal health, balance, and harmony in their lives. The programs include yoga, meditation, fitness, nutrition, and holistic healing therapies such as acupuncture, Ayurveda, and massage.

The retreat's yoga programs are led by experienced teachers who offer classes for all levels, from beginner to advanced. The classes take place in the estate's serene yoga pavilion, overlooking the lush tropical forests and the Ayung River. The meditation programs, on the other hand, are designed to help guests achieve a state of inner peace, clarity, and mindfulness. The retreat's fitness programs include activities such as hiking, cycling, and Pilates, all designed to help guests achieve their fitness goals while enjoying the natural beauty of Bali.

COMO Shambhala Estate's nutrition programs are designed to help guests achieve optimal health through mindful eating. The retreat's menus are carefully crafted to provide guests with delicious and nutritious meals that are tailored to their individual needs. The menus feature organic, locally-sourced ingredients and are inspired by the flavors and traditions of Bali.

Finally, COMO Shambhala Estate's holistic healing therapies are designed to help guests achieve balance and harmony in their lives. The retreat's expert practitioners offer a range of healing therapies, including acupuncture, Ayurveda, and massage, all designed to help guests achieve optimal health and wellbeing.

In conclusion, COMO Shambhala Estate is one of the best wellness retreats in Bali, offering guests a luxurious and serene environment for rejuvenation and relaxation. With its personalized wellness programs, world-class facilities, and exceptional service, the estate provides guests with a truly transformative experience that promotes optimal health, balance, and harmony.

The Yoga Barn, Ubud

The Yoga Barn, located in the heart of Ubud, Bali, is one of the most popular and sought-after wellness retreats in the region. Known for its serene and tranquil atmosphere, world-class facilities, and a wide range of wellness activities, The Yoga Barn is a perfect destination for anyone seeking to rejuvenate their mind, body, and soul.

The Yoga Barn is spread over a vast area of lush green gardens, providing a perfect environment for those seeking inner peace and tranquility. The retreat offers an array of activities including yoga classes, meditation sessions, sound healing, breathwork, and various other holistic therapies. The center hosts more than 100 yoga and meditation classes per week, led by experienced and certified instructors, making it one of the largest yoga centers in Bali.

Apart from the daily yoga classes, The Yoga Barn also offers various workshops, retreats, and teacher training programs throughout the year. These programs are designed to cater to the needs of all levels of practitioners, from beginners to advanced students, and provide a comprehensive learning experience that goes beyond the physical practice of yoga.

One of the unique features of The Yoga Barn is its holistic healing center, KUSH Ayurveda, which offers a range of traditional Ayurvedic treatments, including massage, herbal remedies, and consultations with experienced Ayurvedic practitioners. The retreat also has a raw food cafe that serves delicious and healthy vegetarian and vegan meals made with locally sourced ingredients.

The Yoga Barn has a serene and peaceful environment, which helps visitors to disconnect from the stress and chaos of daily life. The retreat's natural surroundings, including rice paddies, rivers, and jungle landscapes, create a tranquil atmosphere that promotes relaxation and meditation.

The center also offers accommodation options ranging from shared dormitories to private rooms, making it accessible to visitors with different budgets. The retreat's rooms are well-furnished and equipped with modern amenities, providing visitors with a comfortable and relaxing stay.

Fivelements, Mambal

Fivelements is a world-renowned wellness retreat located in Mambal, Bali, Indonesia. This stunning eco-wellness retreat is set amidst lush tropical forests and cascading rice paddies, offering a peaceful and serene environment for guests to rejuvenate their mind, body, and soul.

The concept of Fivelements is inspired by the Balinese philosophy of Tri Hita Karana, which translates to "the three sources of happiness". These sources of happiness include harmony among people, harmony with nature, and harmony with the divine. This philosophy is woven into every aspect of Fivelements, making it a unique and spiritually enriching experience for guests.

The retreat offers a variety of wellness programs designed to restore balance and harmony in the body, mind, and spirit. These programs include yoga and meditation, detox and cleansing, stress relief, rejuvenation, and weight management.

The programs are customized to meet individual needs and are designed to provide a holistic approach to wellness.

Fivelements features state-of-the-art facilities including an open-air bamboo structure that serves as the main wellness center, where guests can enjoy a variety of treatments such as massages, facials, and body scrubs. The retreat also features a beautiful swimming pool, a traditional Balinese kitchen, and a yoga pavilion with stunning views of the surrounding jungle and rice fields.

One of the unique aspects of Fivelements is its commitment to sustainability and environmental conservation. The retreat operates on a zero-waste principle, with all waste being recycled or composted. The retreat also uses organic and locally sourced ingredients in its meals, and promotes sustainable farming practices.

In addition to its wellness programs, Fivelements also offers a range of cultural experiences for guests, including Balinese cooking classes, traditional dance and many more.

Bali Silent Retreat, Tabanan

Bali Silent Retreat in Tabanan is widely considered as one of the best wellness retreats in Bali. The retreat is situated in the heart of Bali's lush jungle and is designed for people who are looking for a peaceful and meditative environment to rejuvenate and recharge their bodies, minds, and souls.

The retreat offers a unique experience for individuals looking to disconnect from the outside world and reconnect with themselves. It provides a sanctuary for individuals to disconnect from the noise and distractions of daily life and reconnect with nature and their inner selves. The retreat promotes silence and self-reflection as a means to connect with one's true essence.

Bali Silent Retreat offers a range of activities and facilities to support the guests in their wellness journey. Some of the activities include meditation, yoga, nature walks, and creative arts. The retreat also offers healthy vegetarian meals made from organic and locally sourced ingredients.

The retreat's accommodations are designed to provide a simple and peaceful environment for the guests. The rooms are built using traditional Balinese architecture and are furnished with comfortable bedding, mosquito nets, and ceiling fans. Each room has a private bathroom and a veranda that overlooks the lush tropical forest.

One of the unique features of Bali Silent Retreat is its commitment to sustainability and environmental conservation. The retreat utilizes renewable energy sources such as solar panels and practices eco-friendly waste management.

The retreat also offers a range of programs that are designed to cater to the individual needs of each guest. Some of the programs include detox and cleansing programs, mindfulness and meditation retreats, and yoga retreats. The retreat's programs are led by experienced and certified wellness practitioners who are dedicated to helping guests achieve their wellness goals.

Bali Silent Retreat has received numerous awards and accolades for its outstanding service and commitment to promoting wellness and sustainability. The retreat has been featured in various travel publications, including Travel + Leisure, Conde Nast Traveler, and National Geographic Traveler.

Bali Silent Retreat in Tabanan is a haven for individuals seeking to disconnect from the outside world and reconnect with themselves.

The retreat's commitment to sustainability, its unique accommodations, and its range of wellness programs make it one of the best wellness retreats in Bali. Whether you are looking to detox and cleanse your body, cultivate mindfulness and meditation, or simply rejuvenate your soul, Bali Silent Retreat offers a transformative experience that will leave you feeling refreshed and renewed.

Svarga Loka Resort, Ubud

Svarga Loka Resort is a wellness retreat located in the heart of Ubud, Bali. It is known as one of the best wellness retreats in Bali due to its world-class facilities, luxurious accommodations, and exceptional staff who provide personalized service to their guests.

Svarga Loka Resort offers a holistic approach to wellness, focusing on the physical, mental, emotional, and spiritual aspects of health. The resort offers a variety of programs and treatments, including yoga, meditation, detox, Ayurveda, acupuncture, and traditional Balinese healing therapies.

The accommodations at Svarga Loka Resort are designed with wellness in mind. The rooms and suites are spacious, comfortable, and equipped with all modern amenities. Each room has a private balcony with a beautiful view of the surrounding lush gardens, rice fields, or jungle. The resort has a variety of room types, including deluxe rooms, suites, villas, and private pool villas, to cater to every guest's needs and preferences.

The resort's facilities are top-notch and designed to enhance the wellness experience of their guests. The resort has a beautiful infinity pool, a state-of-the-art gym, a yoga shala, a meditation hall, and a spa. The spa offers a variety of treatments, including massages, facials, body scrubs, and wraps, using all-natural and organic products.

The food at Svarga Loka Resort is another highlight of the retreat. The resort's restaurant, Pranava, offers delicious and healthy meals made with locally sourced and organic ingredients. The menu is carefully crafted to cater to different dietary requirements, including vegetarian, vegan, gluten-free, and raw food options. The restaurant also offers cooking classes and workshops, where guests can learn to make healthy and nutritious meals.

The staff at Svarga Loka Resort is exceptional and committed to providing personalized service to their guests. The resort's wellness team comprises experienced and certified yoga teachers, meditation teachers, Ayurveda practitioners, and spa therapists, who are passionate about helping guests achieve their wellness goals.

Finally, Svarga Loka Resort is a haven for wellness seekers looking to recharge, rejuvenate, and reconnect with themselves. Its world-class facilities, luxurious accommodations, exceptional staff, and holistic approach to wellness make it one of the best wellness retreats in Bali.

Chapter 6: "Off the Beaten Path: 5 Hidden Gems in Bali Worth Exploring"

Tirta Gangga, a stunning water palace

Tirta Gangga is a breathtaking water palace located in the eastern part of Bali, Indonesia. The palace was built in 1948 by the King of

Karangasem, Anak Agung Anglurah Ketut Karangasem, and is renowned for its stunning gardens, fountains, and pools.

The palace's name, Tirta Gangga, translates to "water from the Ganges," referring to the sacred river in India. The name is fitting, as the palace is built around natural springs and has multiple pools and fountains that are fed by the water. Visitors can take a dip in the pools and experience the refreshing and cool water, which is believed to have healing properties.

The palace is set amidst a serene landscape of lush greenery, with terraced gardens, stone statues, and koi ponds. The grounds are meticulously maintained, with a maze of pathways that lead visitors through different sections of the gardens. One of the most notable features of the palace is the multi-tiered fountain, which rises up to 11 meters high and is surrounded by a ring of twelve smaller fountains.

For those seeking a more peaceful experience, there are several quiet spots throughout the palace grounds that offer stunning views of the surrounding landscape. Visitors can relax in the shade of the pavilions and soak in the tranquil atmosphere, or take a leisurely stroll around the gardens and marvel at the intricate details of the statues and carvings.

Tirta Gangga is not only a popular tourist destination but also an important cultural and historical landmark in Bali. The palace was severely damaged during the eruption of Mount Agung in 1963 but was restored in the 1970s by the Indonesian government. Today, it stands as a testament to Bali's rich cultural heritage and is a must-visit destination for travelers to the island.

Tirta Gangga is a stunning water palace that offers a unique blend of natural beauty and cultural significance. It is a perfect destination for those looking to escape the hustle and bustle of Bali's busy tourist areas and immerse themselves in the island's rich history and culture.

Jatiluwih Rice Terraces, a UNESCO World Heritage Site

Jatiluwih Rice Terraces is a stunning UNESCO World Heritage Site located in the heart of Bali, Indonesia. This beautiful landscape is made up of lush green rice paddies that stretch out over more than 600 hectares of land, with breathtaking views of Bali's volcanic peaks in the distance. Jatiluwih is known for its intricate irrigation system, which has been in use for over 1,000 years and helps to sustain the rice fields.

Visitors to Jatiluwih can experience the beauty and tranquility of traditional Balinese rice farming practices, as well as learn about the intricate systems used to manage the rice terraces. The rice terraces are divided into different levels, with each level being irrigated by a system of canals and dams that have been carefully constructed to ensure that the water flows evenly across the entire area. These systems are maintained by the local farmers, who use traditional techniques to cultivate the rice and manage the land.

One of the best ways to experience the beauty of Jatiluwih is to take a leisurely walk or bike ride through the rice fields. Visitors can take in the stunning views of the terraces and surrounding landscape, while also learning about the history and culture of the area from local guides. There are also several small villages located within the Jatiluwih area, which offer a glimpse into traditional Balinese life and culture.

Jatiluwih is also home to a number of restaurants and cafes, where visitors can enjoy traditional Balinese cuisine made from locally-sourced ingredients. The area is particularly known for its delicious nasi campur (mixed rice dishes), which are often served with fresh vegetables and spices grown in the surrounding rice fields.

Overall, Jatiluwih Rice Terraces is a must-visit destination for travelers to Bali who want to experience the beauty and tranquility of traditional Balinese culture. With its stunning natural landscapes, rich history, and delicious cuisine, Jatiluwih offers a unique and unforgettable travel experience.

Tenganan Village, a preserved Balinese village

Tenganan Village is a hidden gem located in the eastern part of Bali, Indonesia. This traditional Balinese village is nestled among the rolling hills and surrounded by lush green rice fields, making it a picturesque destination for travelers looking to explore the cultural heritage of Bali. The village is well-known for preserving its ancient traditions and customs, and it is considered one of the oldest and most authentic villages in Bali.

One of the most fascinating aspects of Tenganan Village is its strict adherence to the Bali Aga customs and traditions. The Bali Aga people are the original inhabitants of Bali, and they are known for their unique way of life, which is very different from that of the rest of the Balinese population. Visitors can witness the village's traditional architecture, including its unique buffalo-horn-shaped entrances, and observe the locals performing their daily activities, such as weaving, farming, and making intricate handicrafts.

The village's location also offers visitors the opportunity to explore the surrounding areas. Visitors can take a leisurely walk through the rice fields, hike up the hills to enjoy breathtaking views, or simply relax in one of the many cozy cafes and restaurants that dot the area. The village is also conveniently located near popular tourist destinations such as Candidasa Beach, Tirta Gangga Water Palace, and Besakih Temple.

Tenganan Village is a must-visit destination for travelers looking to experience the authentic culture and heritage of Bali. The village's unique customs, stunning natural surroundings, and friendly locals make it a truly unforgettable experience.

Pura Lempuyang, a temple with breathtaking views

Pura Lempuyang, located in East Bali, is a magnificent temple complex that offers breathtaking views of Mount Agung and the surrounding valleys. Known as the "Gateway to Heaven," the temple is perched atop a hill and is accessible only by climbing 1,700 steps, a journey that is well worth the effort. Along the way, visitors will encounter several smaller temples and stunning natural scenery, making it an unforgettable experience. Once at the top, travelers can marvel at the temple's intricate architecture and soak up the stunning panoramic views. For those seeking a spiritual and scenic adventure in Bali, Pura Lempuyang is an absolute must-see.

Menjangan Island, a diving and snorkeling paradise

Menjangan Island is a beautiful and pristine destination for diving and snorkeling in Bali, Indonesia. Located off the northwest coast of Bali, Menjangan Island is part of the Bali Barat National Park and is known for its crystal-clear waters, vibrant coral reefs, and diverse marine life. The island is a haven for divers and snorkelers looking to explore the underwater world and witness the beauty of nature.

Menjangan Island is famous for its wall diving, where divers can descend to depths of up to 60 meters and explore the towering walls of the island's reefs. The waters around Menjangan Island are also home to a wide variety of marine life, including schools of tropical fish, sea turtles, octopuses, and even occasional sightings of whale sharks and manta rays.

For those who prefer snorkeling, Menjangan Island offers an equally impressive experience with shallow reefs just off the beach. The crystal-clear waters make it easy to see the colorful corals and abundant sea life swimming below the surface. The island's calm waters also make it a great destination for beginner divers and snorkelers.

Aside from its underwater attractions, Menjangan Island also boasts stunning white-sand beaches and beautiful landscapes. The island is a popular day trip from Bali, and several tour companies offer snorkeling and diving packages that include transportation, equipment rental, and a guided tour of the island.

Finally,Menjangan Island is a must-visit destination for anyone traveling to Bali who loves diving and snorkeling. With its beautiful coral reefs, diverse marine life, and stunning landscapes, it's easy to see why it's considered a paradise for underwater enthusiasts.

Chapter 7: "Bali with Kids: 5 Fun Family-Friendly Activities"

Bali Safari and Marine Park, Gianyar

Bali Safari and Marine Park in Gianyar is a must-visit destination for travelers to Bali. The park is located amidst the lush greenery of the island, and is home to over 60 species of animals, including elephants, tigers, zebras, and many more. The park offers a unique experience to its visitors, with the opportunity to observe and interact with these magnificent animals in their natural habitats.

The safari journey takes visitors through different habitats, such as the savannah, jungle, and water environments, giving visitors an up-close experience with the animals. The park also offers a range of other attractions, such as the Bali Agung Show, which showcases Bali's rich culture and history through dance, music, and acrobatics. There is also a water park, where visitors can cool off and enjoy thrilling water slides and other attractions.

One of the highlights of the Bali Safari and Marine Park is the opportunity to have breakfast with the lions, where visitors can dine while watching the lions in their enclosure. For those looking for an even closer encounter, the park also offers elephant and camel rides.

Overall, the Bali Safari and Marine Park offers a unique and exciting experience for travelers to Bali. With its combination of animal encounters, cultural attractions, and water park, it is an excellent destination for families and solo travelers alike

Waterbom Bali, Kuta

Waterbom Bali is one of the most popular water parks in Bali, located in the heart of Kuta. It is an exciting destination for travelers looking for a fun-filled day with family and friends. With over 20 water rides, slides, and attractions, Waterbom Bali offers something for everyone.

The park is well-designed and maintained, with lush greenery and landscaping, making it a perfect escape from the busy streets of Kuta. Visitors can choose from thrilling rides such as the Python, Climax, and Superbowl, or relax in the lazy river or one of the many pools available.

One of the highlights of Waterbom Bali is the Flow Rider, which offers an artificial wave that's perfect for surfing enthusiasts. Other attractions include the Water Blaster, which propels riders up a steep incline before dropping them down a steep drop, and the Constrictor, which sends riders down a series of tight, twisting tubes.

Waterbom Bali also offers a variety of food and beverage options, including several restaurants and snack bars. Visitors can enjoy Indonesian cuisine, as well as western favorites such as burgers and pizza. The park also offers a variety of facilities, including lockers, showers, and changing rooms.

Overall, Waterbom Bali is a must-visit destination for travelers to Bali, offering an exciting day out for visitors of all ages. Whether you're seeking a thrill or just want to relax and soak up the sun, Waterbom Bali has something for everyone.

Bali Treetop Adventure Park, Bedugul:

For travelers seeking adventure and thrill, Bali Treetop Adventure Park in Bedugul is a must-visit destination. Nestled amidst the lush green forests of Bali, the adventure park offers a wide range of activities for visitors of all ages. The park features six adventure circuits, with over 72 challenges and obstacles, including suspended bridges, spider nets, flying foxes, and many more.

The park is suitable for families, groups, or individual travelers who are seeking a fun and exhilarating experience. The activities are supervised by trained professionals who prioritize the safety of the visitors. The park also provides all the necessary equipment, including helmets, gloves, and harnesses.

In addition to the adventure circuits, the park also offers an impressive view of the Bedugul Botanical Garden and Lake Bratan. Visitors can also take a leisurely stroll through the gardens and enjoy the fresh air and natural surroundings.

Bali Bird Park, Gianyar:

Bali Bird Park is a fantastic attraction for nature and bird enthusiasts visiting the island of Bali. The park is home to over 1000 birds from over 250 different species, including rare and endangered species such as the Bali Starling and the Javan Kingfisher.

The park is designed to provide a natural environment for the birds, with spacious aviaries, gardens, and ponds that replicate the birds' natural habitats. Visitors can enjoy a guided tour of the park or explore it on their own. The park also offers interactive shows and educational presentations to learn more about the birds and their habitats.

Apart from the birds, the park also features a restaurant, a gift shop, and a children's playground. It is an ideal destination for families, couples, or individual travelers who are looking for a unique and educational experience.

Green Camp Bali, Ubud:

Green Camp Bali is a sustainable learning center and eco-resort located in the heart of Ubud. The camp offers a range of programs and activities that promote sustainability, environmental education, and community building.

The camp offers a variety of programs and activities, including organic farming, bamboo building, natural dyes, and composting. Visitors can also enjoy yoga, meditation, and other wellness activities, as well as outdoor adventures such as hiking and rafting.

The accommodations at Green Camp Bali are eco-friendly and designed to provide a comfortable and sustainable living experience. Visitors can choose from various options, including bamboo huts, safari tents, and tree houses.

Green Camp Bali is an excellent destination for travelers who are interested in sustainability, eco-tourism, and outdoor adventures. The camp offers a unique and immersive experience that allows visitors to connect with nature and learn more about sustainable living practices.

Chapter 8: "Bali's Nightlife Scene: 5 Hotspots for a Night Out"

Potato Head Beach Club, Seminyak

Potato Head Beach Club is one of the most iconic and popular destinations for travelers visiting the beautiful island of Bali in Indonesia. Located in the heart of Seminyak, this luxury beach club offers an unparalleled experience that combines world-class entertainment, delectable dining, and stunning ocean views.

The Potato Head Beach Club is known for its stunning design and architecture, which seamlessly blends traditional Balinese elements with modern touches. The club's centerpiece is an impressive amphitheater-style infinity pool that overlooks the Indian Ocean, providing guests with a breathtaking backdrop as they relax and unwind.

One of the main draws of the Potato Head Beach Club is its lively atmosphere, which is perfect for travelers looking for a fun and social experience. With a capacity of up to 2,500 people, the club regularly hosts some of the biggest parties and events in Bali, featuring renowned DJs and performers from around the world.

In addition to its vibrant nightlife scene, the Potato Head Beach Club is also a great place to enjoy a day out in the sun. The club's beachfront location means that guests have direct access to the beautiful Seminyak Beach, where they can enjoy swimming, sunbathing, and a range of water sports.

The food and drink options at the Potato Head Beach Club are also second to none, with a range of restaurants and bars serving up delicious cuisine from around the world. From freshly caught seafood to gourmet burgers and pizzas, there is something to suit all tastes and preferences.

For those looking for a more exclusive experience, the Potato Head Beach Club also offers a range of private cabanas and lounges that provide a more intimate setting for enjoying the club's offerings. These luxurious spaces are equipped with all the amenities one could need, including private showers, air conditioning, and personalized service from dedicated staff.

Overall, the Potato Head Beach Club is a must-visit destination for anyone traveling to Bali. Whether you're looking to party the night away, soak up the sun on the beach, or indulge in some delicious food and drink, this iconic beach club has something for everyone.

Sky Garden, Kuta

Sky Garden is a popular nightclub and dining spot located in the bustling area of Kuta, Bali. The venue offers an exciting mix of dining, entertainment, and nightlife, making it a must-visit for travelers looking to experience the vibrant energy of Bali's nightlife scene.

As you step into Sky Garden, you'll be greeted by a stylish, modern interior that's designed to create a lively and inviting atmosphere. The venue has multiple levels, each with its own distinct ambiance, including a rooftop bar that offers stunning views of the city.

One of the main draws of Sky Garden is its extensive menu of international cuisine. From local Indonesian dishes to Western favorites, the food here is always fresh and delicious. Whether you're looking for a quick snack or a full meal, Sky Garden has something to satisfy every taste bud.

As the night goes on, the venue transforms into a high-energy nightclub, with top local and international DJs spinning the latest dance hits. The dance floor is always packed with locals and tourists alike, making it a great place to meet new people and let loose.

Overall, Sky Garden is a must-visit spot for travelers looking to experience the best of Bali's nightlife scene. With its delicious food, stunning views, and exciting entertainment, it's the perfect place to party the night away

La Favela, Seminyak

La Favela is one of the most popular nightclubs in Bali, located in the bustling area of Seminyak. It has become a must-visit destination for travelers looking to experience the nightlife scene in Bali.

La Favela boasts a unique concept and decor that takes inspiration from the urban landscape of

Brazil's favelas. The nightclub's interior is adorned with vintage furniture, graffiti murals, and colorful tiles, which add to its vibrant and lively atmosphere.

The music at La Favela is another major drawcard. The nightclub features a wide range of music genres, including Latin, reggae, house, and hip-hop. DJs from all over the world take to the decks at La Favela, playing the latest hits and timeless classics, ensuring that there is something for everyone.

One of the standout features of La Favela is its extensive cocktail menu. The nightclub has a team of skilled mixologists who create signature cocktails using local ingredients and exotic flavors. From classic mojitos to creative concoctions, La Favela's drinks menu is sure to satisfy even the most discerning cocktail connoisseurs.

La Favela's outdoor area is also a great place to relax and enjoy the evening breeze. The outdoor space is adorned with colorful fairy lights, creating a cozy and intimate atmosphere. It's the perfect spot to enjoy a drink or two while taking in the lively atmosphere of the nightclub.

One of the reasons why La Favela is so popular among travelers to Bali is its welcoming and inclusive atmosphere. The nightclub attracts a diverse crowd, including locals, expats, and tourists, creating a melting pot of cultures and nationalities. Whether you're traveling solo or with friends, La Favela is a great place to meet new people and make lasting memories.

La Favela is a must-visit destination for travelers looking for an unforgettable night out in Bali. With its unique concept and decor, diverse music selection, extensive cocktail menu, and welcoming atmosphere, La Favela is sure to deliver an experience that you won't forget

Single Fin, Uluwatu

Single Fin, Uluwatu is one of the best night out spots in Bali. It is situated on the southern tip of Bali, perched on a cliff overlooking the Indian Ocean. Single Fin is a popular spot for surfers, tourists, and locals alike who come to enjoy the stunning views, delicious food, and lively atmosphere.

As the name suggests, Single Fin is a surf bar that pays homage to the iconic single fin surfboards of the 70s. The bar has a laid-back vibe with surfboards and memorabilia decorating the walls, and a large outdoor seating area that overlooks the ocean. The sunsets at Single Fin are simply breathtaking, making it the perfect spot to relax with a cold beer or cocktail.

When the sun goes down, the bar comes to life with live music, DJs, and dancing. The music ranges from reggae to house, and the crowd is a mix of locals and tourists. The atmosphere is electric, with everyone enjoying the music and the beautiful surroundings.

Single Fin also offers delicious food that is perfect for a night out. The menu features a mix of Western and Indonesian cuisine, with everything from pizzas and burgers to nasi goreng and satay. The bar also serves a range of cocktails and beers, with happy hour specials that make it easy to enjoy a night out without breaking the bank.

In addition to its nightlife, Single Fin is also a popular spot for surfing. The bar is situated right above Uluwatu Beach, which is known for its world-class waves. Surfers come from all over the world to ride the waves at Uluwatu, and Single Fin is the perfect place to watch them in action.

Single Fin, Uluwatu is a must-visit spot for anyone looking for a fun night out in Bali. The stunning views, delicious food, and lively atmosphere make it the perfect place to relax, socialize, and dance the night away. Whether you're a surfer or not, Single Fin is a great spot to experience the best of Bali's nightlife.

Chapter 9: "Romantic Bali: 5 Activities for Couples"

Sunset dinner at Jimbaran Bay

A sunset dinner at Jimbaran Bay is an ideal couple activity in Bali. Jimbaran Bay is located on the southern coast of Bali and is renowned for its stunning sunsets and fresh seafood. It is an ideal place for couples to unwind, enjoy the tranquil ambiance, and relish some of the most delectable seafood dishes. The setting is perfect for a romantic date and an excellent way to experience the beauty of Bali.

Jimbaran Bay is home to several seafood restaurants that offer fresh seafood caught from the bay itself. The local fishermen bring in their catch every morning, and the restaurants display the fresh catch of the day for customers to select their favorite seafood. Couples can choose their seafood, and it is then prepared and cooked to their liking, making it a personalized dining experience.

The restaurants at Jimbaran Bay are designed in such a way that couples can enjoy the breathtaking views of the sunset while savoring their food. The tables are set up on the beach, and couples can dine with their feet in the sand and the waves lapping at their toes. The atmosphere is incredibly romantic, and the sound of the waves crashing against the shore is an added bonus to the experience.

The seafood at Jimbaran Bay is renowned for its freshness, and the flavors are unique to the region. The dishes are prepared in a simple yet flavorful manner, with a focus on the freshness of the seafood. Grilled fish, squid, prawns, and lobsters are some of the seafood dishes that are commonly served at the restaurants. These are accompanied by rice, vegetables, and sambal, a spicy Indonesian sauce.

The sunset at Jimbaran Bay is undoubtedly the highlight of the experience. The sky transforms into a stunning display of colors, with hues of orange, pink, and purple painting the horizon. As the sun dips below the horizon, the atmosphere becomes even more romantic, with the twinkling lights of the fishing boats in the bay adding to the charm.

In addition to the sunset dinner, there are other activities couples can enjoy at Jimbaran Bay. The beach is perfect for an evening stroll, and couples can enjoy the cool breeze while walking hand in hand. There are also several water sports activities available for the adventurous couple, including surfing, parasailing, and jet skiing

A sunset dinner at Jimbaran Bay is an unforgettable experience and an ideal couple activity in Bali. The combination of fresh seafood, stunning sunsets, and the romantic atmosphere makes it the perfect date night for couples. The experience offers an excellent way to unwind, relax, and connect with your significant other, making it a must-do activity when in Bali.

Sunrise hike to Mount Batur

One of the most popular activities for couples visiting Bali is a sunrise hike to Mount Batur.

Mount Batur is an active volcano located in the north of Bali, and it is one of the island's most popular hiking destinations. The hike to the summit of Mount Batur takes around two to three hours and is usually done early in the morning to catch the stunning sunrise views.

The sunrise hike to Mount Batur is a perfect couple activity in Bali, as it offers a unique and memorable experience. The hike provides couples with an opportunity to witness the stunning views of the sunrise over the ocean and the beautiful landscape of Bali. As you hike up the mountain, you will pass through lush green forests, small villages, and farms, giving you a glimpse of Bali's rural life.

The hike is also a perfect opportunity for couples to bond and spend quality time together. The trek can be quite challenging, and it requires a good level of fitness, so couples can support and motivate each other along the way. The feeling of accomplishment when you reach the summit together will strengthen your relationship and create lasting memories.

To prepare for the sunrise hike, couples should wear comfortable and sturdy shoes, bring plenty of water, and wear appropriate clothing for the cooler temperatures at the summit. It is also recommended to bring a camera to capture the stunning views and a headlamp or flashlight for the early morning hike.

The hike to Mount Batur is usually done with a guide who will lead you along the way and provide you with insights into the local culture and history. After reaching the summit, you can enjoy a hot breakfast while taking in the stunning views of the sunrise and the surrounding landscape.

In conclusion, a sunrise hike to Mount Batur is a perfect couple activity in Bali that offers a unique and memorable experience. The stunning views, the challenging trek, and the opportunity to bond and spend quality time together make it a perfect way to start your day in Bali. So, if you are planning a trip to Bali, don't forget to add the sunrise hike to Mount Batur to your itinerary

Couples massage at a luxury spa

One of the most popular couple activities in Bali is a couples massage at a luxury spa. This indulgent experience offers a romantic and relaxing escape for couples to bond and rejuvenate.

Bali is famous for its luxury spas, which offer a range of massages and treatments using traditional Balinese techniques and natural ingredients. Couples can choose from a variety of spa packages, which typically include a private room for two, a personalized massage, and additional services such as aromatherapy, body scrubs, and facial treatments.

The experience of a couples massage starts with a warm welcome from the spa's receptionists, who will guide you through the spa's amenities and services. The staff will then escort you to your private room, where you will find a comfortable massage table, soft lighting, and relaxing music. The room is often decorated with fragrant flowers and candles, creating a romantic ambiance that is perfect for couples.

The massage itself is a soothing and calming experience, designed to relax the body and mind. The therapist will use a combination of techniques, including long strokes, kneading, and gentle stretching, to release tension and improve circulation. They will also use a blend of natural oils and aromatherapy to enhance the massage's therapeutic benefits and create a blissful atmosphere.

The couples massage is a great way for couples to spend quality time together and reconnect. The shared experience of relaxation and rejuvenation creates a sense of intimacy and trust, and helps to strengthen the bond between partners. It also provides an opportunity for couples to unwind and forget about the stresses of daily life, allowing them to fully immerse themselves in the moment and each other's company.

After the massage, couples can enjoy a variety of additional services, such as hot tubs, saunas, and steam rooms. Some spas also offer private outdoor areas where couples can relax and enjoy the stunning Balinese scenery. They can also indulge in a variety of healthy snacks and beverages, such as fresh fruit juices and herbal teas.

In addition to the physical and emotional benefits of a couples massage, it also provides an opportunity to explore Bali's rich cultural heritage. Many spas incorporate traditional Balinese elements into their treatments, such as the use of natural herbs, spices, and oils. Couples can also learn more about Balinese culture and customs by attending workshops and classes offered by the spa.

A couples massage at a luxury spa is an unforgettable experience that offers a perfect blend of relaxation, romance, and cultural immersion. It is a great way for couples to bond and rejuvenate while exploring one of the most beautiful and exotic destinations in the world. With its stunning natural beauty, rich cultural heritage, and luxurious amenities, Bali is the perfect destination for a romantic getaway

Private Villa with a Pool:

Bali offers a plethora of luxurious private villas with pools, providing the ultimate romantic hideaway. Imagine waking up to the sound of the gentle waves, surrounded by lush greenery and tropical flowers. A private villa with a pool offers a sense of seclusion and intimacy that cannot be found in hotels or resorts.

The villas range from intimate one-bedroom to expansive multi-bedroom properties, each with their unique charm and amenities. Most villas feature an open living and dining area, fully equipped kitchen, and a private garden with a pool. Some villas also have a private spa, gym, cinema room, or even a tennis court.

Spending time in a private villa with a pool provides an opportunity to relax and unwind, enjoying each other's company in complete privacy. Imagine soaking in your private pool while sipping on a tropical cocktail, enjoying the warmth of the Balinese sun. You can also order in-room massages, private chef services, or take a cooking class to learn the art of Balinese cuisine.

Scenic Helicopter Tour of Bali:

For a breathtaking view of Bali, take a scenic helicopter tour. A helicopter tour allows you to see the island's natural beauty from a unique perspective, with panoramic views of the lush rice paddies, towering volcanoes, and turquoise waters.

The helicopter tour can be customized to your preferences, with various packages available to suit different interests and budgets. You can choose to fly over Bali's iconic landmarks such as Mount Agung, Tanah Lot Temple, and the Ubud rice terraces. You can also opt for a private beach picnic, where the helicopter lands on a secluded beach, and you can enjoy a romantic picnic lunch.

A helicopter tour provides a once-in-a-lifetime experience, allowing you to see the beauty of Bali in a way that cannot be replicated. It is a perfect activity for couples who want to add some adventure and excitement to their romantic getaway.

Renting a private villa with a pool and taking a scenic helicopter tour are two fantastic activities that can enhance your romantic getaway in Bali. The combination of seclusion, luxury, and breathtaking scenery will create memories that will last a lifetime.

Chapter 10: The Best Souvenirs to Bring Home from Bali: 5 Must-Buy Items.

Batik textiles and clothing

One of the most prominent and sought-after aspects of Balinese culture is Batik textiles and clothing. Batik is a traditional Indonesian fabric that has been hand-dyed and decorated for centuries. Bali is famous for producing some of the finest Batik textiles and clothing in the world. If you are planning a trip to Bali, then Batik textiles and clothing are a must-buy souvenir to take home with you.

Batik is an ancient art form that has been passed down from generation to generation in Indonesia. It involves the application of wax to fabric to create intricate patterns and designs. The fabric is then dyed, and the wax is removed, revealing the design underneath. This process can be repeated several times, creating intricate layers of color and pattern. The result is a beautiful and unique textile that is perfect for clothing, home décor, or even wall hangings.

In Bali, you will find a wide range of Batik textiles and clothing. From simple scarves and sarongs to elaborate dresses and blouses, there is something for everyone. The quality of Batik produced in Bali is exceptional, with skilled artisans using traditional techniques to create stunning designs. You will find a wide range of colors, patterns, and designs, from bold and bright to subtle and understated.

One of the best places to find Batik textiles and clothing in Bali is in the Ubud market. Here, you will find a plethora of vendors selling a range of Batik products. From small trinkets and souvenirs to elaborate dresses and blouses, there is something for everyone. You can haggle with the vendors to get the best price, and many of them will offer to create custom designs for you.

When shopping for Batik textiles and clothing in Bali, it is important to look for authentic products. There are many mass-produced Batik products that are not made using traditional techniques or materials. These products may be cheaper, but they lack the quality and authenticity of true Batik textiles. Look for Batik that is handmade, using traditional techniques and materials, and be prepared to pay a little more for the real thing.

Batik textiles and clothing are a must-buy souvenir when visiting Bali. They are a beautiful and unique reminder of the rich culture and traditions of this Indonesian island. Whether you are looking for a simple scarf or an elaborate dress, you will find a wide range of Batik products in Bali. Look for authentic products that are handmade using traditional techniques and materials, and be prepared to pay a little more for the real thing

Handmade jewelry and accessories

Bali is a paradise for travelers seeking unique and exotic experiences, from stunning landscapes to rich cultural heritage. One of the most remarkable aspects of Bali is its vibrant art scene, with traditional crafts and handmade goods widely available throughout the island. Among these treasures, handmade jewelry and accessories stand out as must-buy items for any visitor to Bali.

Handmade jewelry and accessories in Bali are known for their intricate designs, high-quality materials, and affordable prices. The Balinese have a long history of creating beautiful pieces of jewelry, often using traditional techniques passed down through generations. These techniques involve intricate carving, weaving, and metalwork, resulting in stunning pieces of jewelry that are both beautiful and unique.

Some of the most popular materials used in handmade jewelry in Bali include silver, gold, precious and semi-precious stones, wood, bone, and leather. Each of these materials has its unique properties and is often combined to create one-of-a-kind pieces that reflect the Balinese culture and artistry.

When it comes to shopping for handmade jewelry in Bali, there are many options available. You can visit one of the many local markets, such as the Ubud Art Market or the Sukawati Art Market, where you can find a wide range of jewelry and accessories from different artisans. You can also visit some of the many jewelry shops and boutiques in Bali, many of which specialize in unique and high-quality handmade pieces.

One of the benefits of buying handmade jewelry in Bali is the opportunity to meet and interact with the artisans who create these pieces. Many Balinese jewelry makers are happy to share their knowledge and expertise with visitors, explaining their techniques and materials used in their craft. This interaction adds to the overall experience of buying handmade jewelry in Bali, providing a deeper appreciation for the art form and the culture behind it.

In addition to traditional Balinese jewelry, Bali is also known for its modern and contemporary designs, blending traditional techniques with new materials and styles. Some of these modern designs incorporate eco-friendly and sustainable materials, such as recycled glass and bamboo, further showcasing the Balinese commitment to preserving the environment.

Handmade jewelry and accessories are a must-buy item for any visitor to Bali, offering a unique and beautiful reminder of the island's vibrant culture and art scene. With its rich history of traditional craftsmanship and modern design, Bali has something to offer for every style and taste. Whether you're looking for a special gift or a piece of jewelry to add to your collection, Bali is the perfect destination to find beautiful and unique handmade jewelry and accessories

Traditional Balinese masks and puppets

Balinese traditional masks and puppets are an integral part of Balinese culture and art, and they are highly valued by locals and tourists alike.

Balinese masks and puppets are typically used in traditional Balinese performances and ceremonies, such as the Barong dance, the Wayang Kulit shadow puppet show, and the Topeng dance. These performances often depict Balinese myths and legends, and the masks and puppets serve as a way to bring these stories to life.

Balinese masks are often carved out of wood, and they feature intricate designs and vibrant colors. They are used to represent different characters in traditional Balinese performances, such as the Barong, a mythical creature that represents good, and the Rangda, a demon queen who represents evil.

Balinese puppets, on the other hand, are typically made out of leather or other materials, and they are used in shadow puppet shows. These shows are typically accompanied by gamelan music, and they tell the stories of Balinese myths and legends. The puppeteers manipulate the puppets behind a screen, creating intricate shadow plays that are both captivating and mesmerizing.

If you're planning a trip to Bali, traditional Balinese masks and puppets are a must-buy souvenir. They make for a unique and memorable gift, and they are a great way to bring a piece of Balinese culture and art into your home.

When shopping for Balinese masks and puppets, it's important to look for authentic pieces that are handcrafted by local artisans. Many of the masks and puppets sold in tourist areas are mass-produced and lack the authenticity and craftsmanship of true Balinese art.

To ensure that you're getting an authentic Balinese mask or puppet, look for pieces that are made from high-quality materials and feature intricate designs and vibrant colors. You can also look for pieces that are signed or marked by the artist, as this can add value and authenticity to your purchase.

Traditional Balinese masks and puppets are a must-buy souvenir for anyone visiting Bali. They are a beautiful and unique representation of Balinese culture and art, and they make for a wonderful addition to any home or collection. When shopping for Balinese masks and puppets, be sure to look for authentic pieces that are handcrafted by local artisans, and you're sure to bring home a truly special souvenir

Coffee and spices from Bali

Bali is a popular tourist destination located in Indonesia. Known for its beautiful beaches, cultural sites, and lush greenery, Bali also offers an array of exotic and flavorful products that are a must-buy for anyone visiting the island. Among these products, coffee and spices are highly recommended for their unique taste and quality.

Bali is famous for its coffee, which is grown on the island's fertile volcanic soil. One of the most famous types of Balinese coffee is Kopi Luwak, also known as civet coffee. This coffee is made from beans that have been eaten and excreted by civet cats, then harvested and processed by farmers. Kopi Luwak is known for its smooth, rich flavor and is considered one of the most expensive coffees in the world. However, there are also other varieties of coffee available in Bali, such as Arabica, Robusta, and Bali Kintamani coffee, which are all worth trying and make great souvenirs to bring back home.

In addition to coffee, Bali is also known for its spices. Spices have been an essential part of Balinese cuisine for centuries and are used to add flavor and aroma to dishes. One of the most popular spices in Bali is turmeric, which is used in many traditional Balinese dishes such as yellow rice and chicken satay. Other popular spices in Bali include cinnamon, nutmeg, and clove, which are often used in sweet dishes such as cakes and desserts.

When shopping for coffee and spices in Bali, there are several markets and shops that offer a wide range of products. One of the most popular places to buy coffee and spices is at the Ubud Market, located in the heart of Ubud. Here, visitors can find a variety of products ranging from coffee beans and ground coffee to various spices and seasonings. The market also offers an array of other Balinese souvenirs such as handicrafts, clothing, and jewelry.

Another popular place to buy coffee and spices in Bali is at the Bali Pulina coffee plantation, located in the village of Tegallalang. Here, visitors can learn about the process of making Balinese coffee, as well as sample different varieties of coffee and purchase products to take home. The plantation also offers a stunning view of the surrounding rice terraces, making it a great place to relax and enjoy a cup of coffee.

Bali is a treasure trove of exotic and flavorful products, and coffee and spices are definitely among the must-buy items when visiting the island. With its rich soil, diverse climate, and traditional farming methods, Bali produces some of the finest coffee and spices in the world, and bringing home these products is a great way to share the unique flavors of Bali with friends and family.

Hand-carved wooden souvenirs and home decor.

Bali, the Island of the Gods, is known for its picturesque landscapes, beautiful beaches, and rich culture. However, Bali is also famous for its hand-carved wooden souvenirs and home decor. These handcrafted items are not only beautiful but also reflect the island's rich cultural heritage. In this note, we will discuss why hand-carved wooden souvenirs and home decor are a must-buy in Bali.

Bali's wood carving tradition dates back centuries, and Balinese craftsmen are renowned for their skills in this art form. They create intricate designs that reflect the island's rich cultural heritage, including gods and goddesses, mythical creatures, and scenes from Balinese life. The wood used in these carvings is usually teak, a dense and durable wood that can withstand the humid climate of the island.

One of the most popular wooden souvenirs in Bali is the wooden mask. These masks are traditionally used in Balinese dance performances and are believed to represent various gods and goddesses. The masks are intricately carved and painted in vibrant colors, making them a stunning addition to any home decor.

Another popular item is the wooden statue. Balinese craftsmen create stunning statues of gods and goddesses, mythical creatures, and animals. These statues are often used in Balinese temples and are believed to bring good luck and fortune to the home.

Wooden boxes and containers are also popular souvenirs in Bali. These boxes are intricately carved with traditional Balinese designs and are perfect for storing jewelry or other small items.

One of the most unique wooden souvenirs in Bali is the wooden egg. These eggs are intricately carved and painted with traditional

Balinese designs. They are believed to bring good luck and are often given as gifts during weddings and other special occasions.

In addition to souvenirs, Balinese craftsmen also create stunning wooden home decor items. One of the most popular items is the wooden panel. These panels are intricately carved and can be used as a room divider or as a wall hanging.

Wooden furniture is also a popular home decor item in Bali. Balinese craftsmen create stunning wooden chairs, tables, and bed frames. These pieces are not only beautiful but also functional and durable.

Hand-carved wooden souvenirs and home decor are a must-buy in Bali. These items reflect the island's rich cultural heritage and are a beautiful addition to any home. Balinese craftsmen are renowned for their skills in woodcarving, and the intricate designs and vibrant colors of these items are a testament to their talent. If you're visiting Bali, be sure to take home a piece of this island paradise in the form of a hand-carved wooden souvenir or home decor item.

Printed in Great Britain
by Amazon